THE BEATLES BOOK
FOR CLASSICAL GUITAR

THE BEATLES BOOK FOR CLASSICAL GUITAR

KIDS EDITION

Arranged by Javier Marcó

The Beatles Book for Classical Guitar – Kids Edition

Licensed by:
Publishing House of the Musical Catalogue of The Beatles:
Sony/ATV Music Publishing (Northern Songs)
All rights reserved

© 2010 by Javier Marcó. All rights reserved.
© 2010 Illustrations by Eugenia Pereyra. All rights reserved.

Unauthorized reproduction of any part of this publication by any means including photocopying is an infringement of copyright.

CONTENTS

- PRELIMINARY NOTES 9
- PLAYING GUIDE 10
- SONGS IN STANDARD NOTATION AND TAB
- ACROSS THE UNIVERSE 12
- ALL MY LOVING 14
- EIGHT DAYS A WEEK 16
- FOR NO ONE 18
- HELP! 20
- I WANT TO HOLD YOUR HAND 22
- I'LL FOLLOW THE SUN 24
- IN MY LIFE 26
- IT'S ONLY LOVE 28
- LUCY IN THE SKY WITH DIAMONDS 30
- NOWHERE MAN 32
- SHE'S LEAVING HOME 34
- THE LONG AND WINDING ROAD 36
- WHILE MY GUITAR GENTLY WEEPS 38
- YELLOW SUBMARINE 40

SONGS IN STANDARD NOTATION

ACROSS THE UNIVERSE 45

ALL MY LOVING 46

EIGHT DAYS A WEEK 47

FOR NO ONE 48

HELP! 49

I WANT TO HOLD YOUR HAND 50

I'LL FOLLOW THE SUN 52

IT'S ONLY LOVE 53

IN MY LIFE 54

LUCY IN THE SKY WITH DIAMONDS 56

NOWHERE MAN 58

SHE'S LEAVING HOME 60

THE LONG AND WINDING ROAD 62

WHILE MY GUITAR GENTLY WEEPS 64

YELLOW SUBMARINE 66

PRELIMINARY NOTES

The 15 songs included in this book have been arranged for classical guitar in first position, to be played by kids as well as beginner level guitar players.

The songs can be also played on two guitars, one player using the notes of the upper register and the second player the notes of the lower register.

Enjoy!

PLAYING GUIDE

-Fingering

Left Hand
0 = open string
1 = index
2 = middle
3 = ring
4 = little finger

Right Hand
p = thumb
i = index
m = middle
a = ring

-Roman numbers indicates fret position for bars
CI = full bar, first fret.
cII = half bar, second fret.

Solid lines indicates how long to hold the bar.

-Repeat sign
The repeat sign indicates a section should be repeated from the beginning, and then continue on. A corresponding sign facing the other way indicates where the repeat is to begin.

 Repeat sign

-First and second endings
The section should be repeated from the beginning, and number brackets above the bars indicate which to played the first time (1), which to play the second time (2).

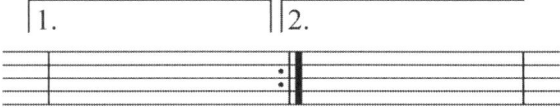

-Repeats

Da Capo is a musical term in Italian meaning *from the beginning*. It is often abbreviated **D.C.**

D.C. al fine repeat from the beginning up to the word **fine**.

Dal Segno is a musical term in Italian meaning *from the sign*. It is often abbreviated **D.S.**

D.S. al Coda repeat back to the sign, and when **To Coda** is reached jump to the coda symbol.

𝄋 the Sign   ⊕ the Coda symbol

Across the Universe

Lennon/McCartney
Arr. by Javier Marco

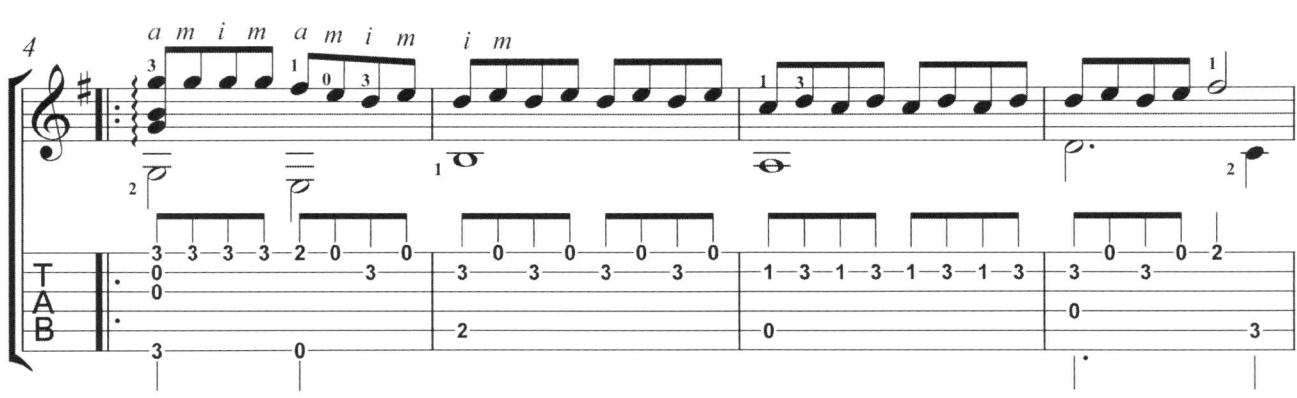
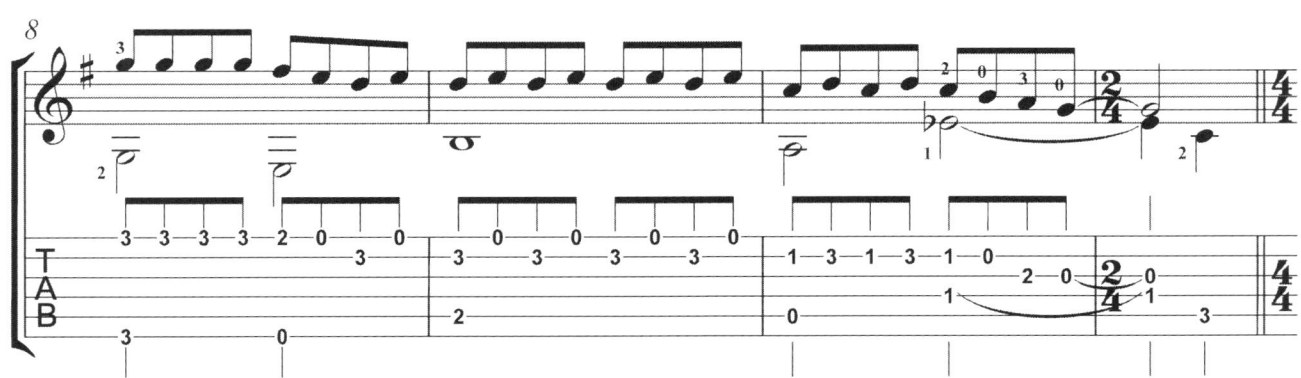

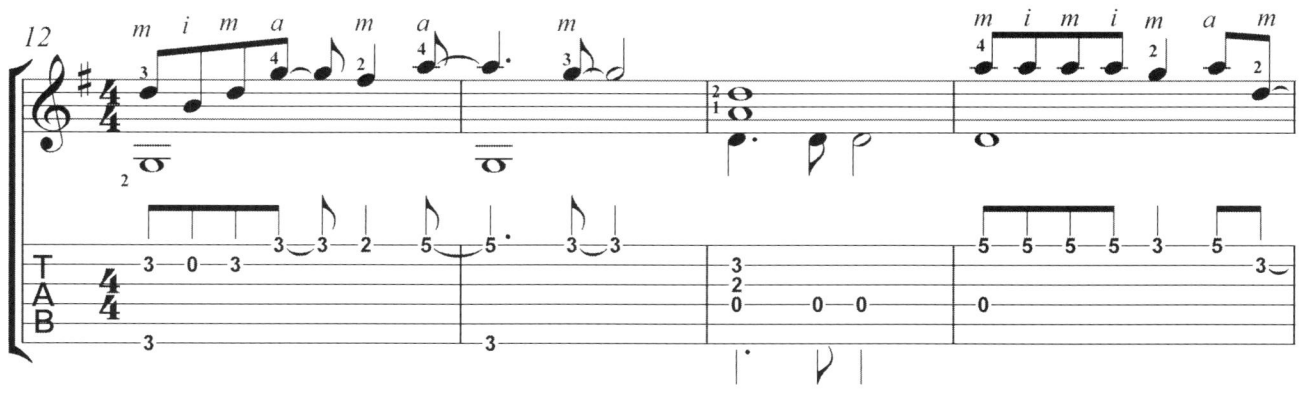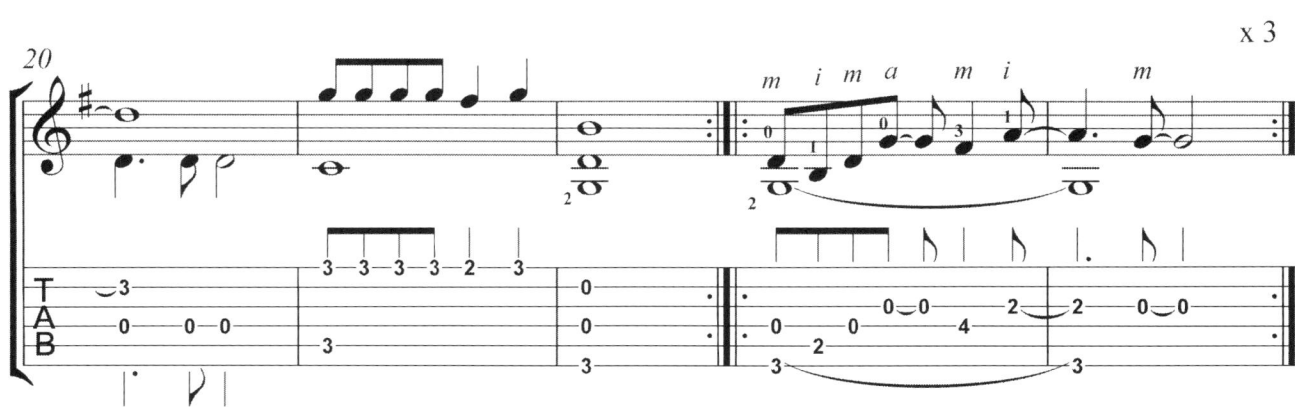

All My Loving

Lennon/McCartney
Arr. by Javier Marco

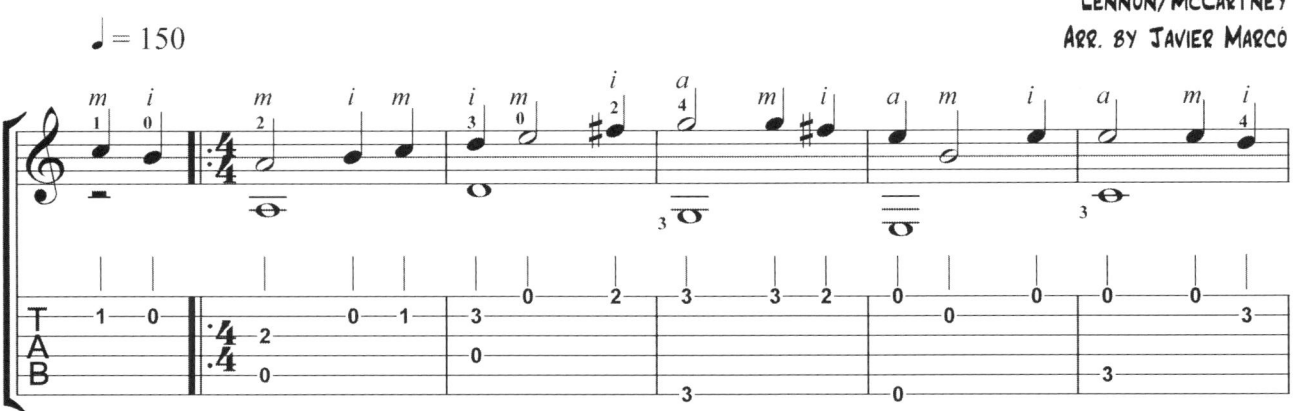

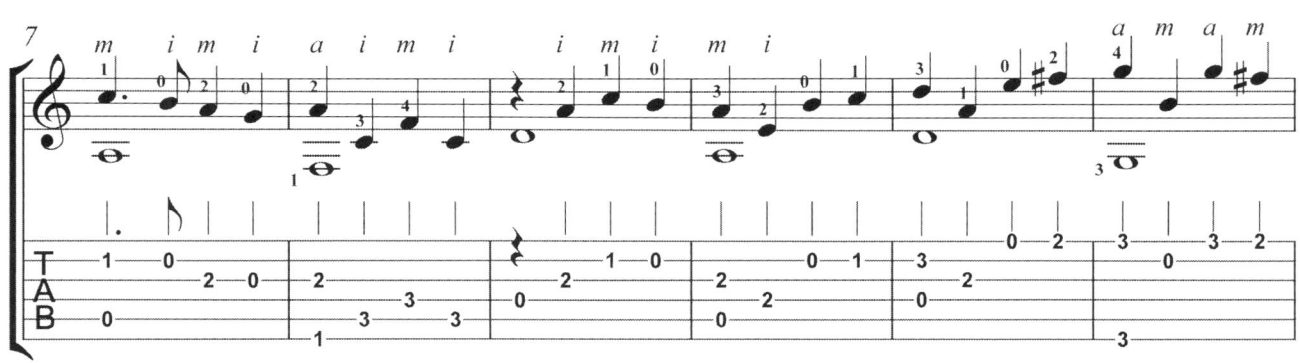

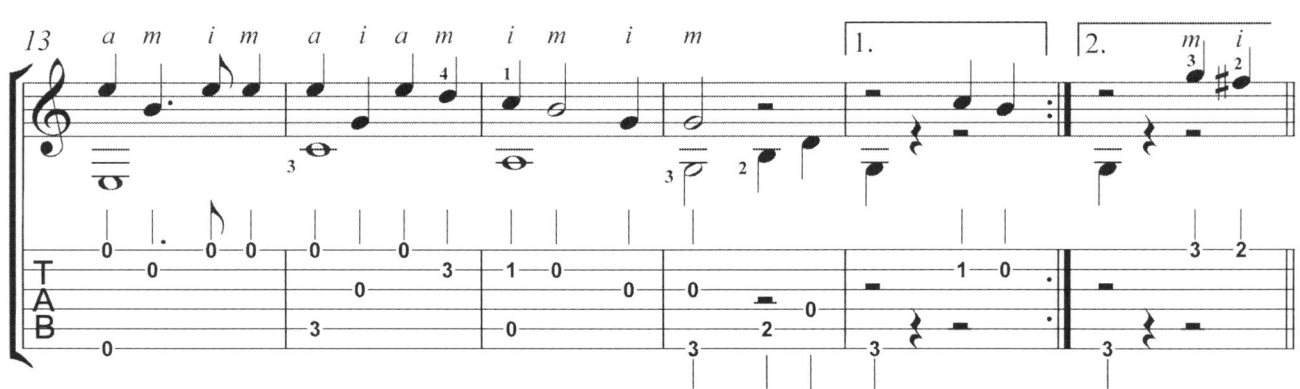

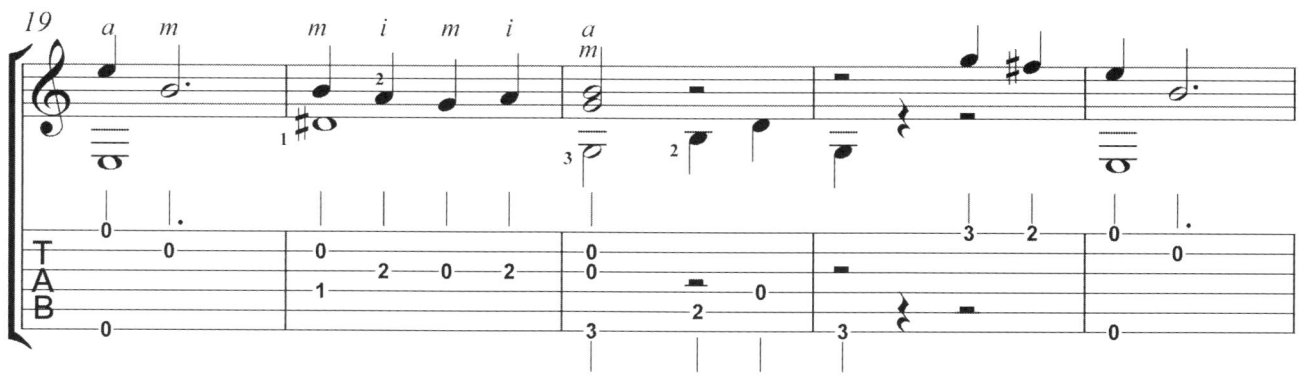
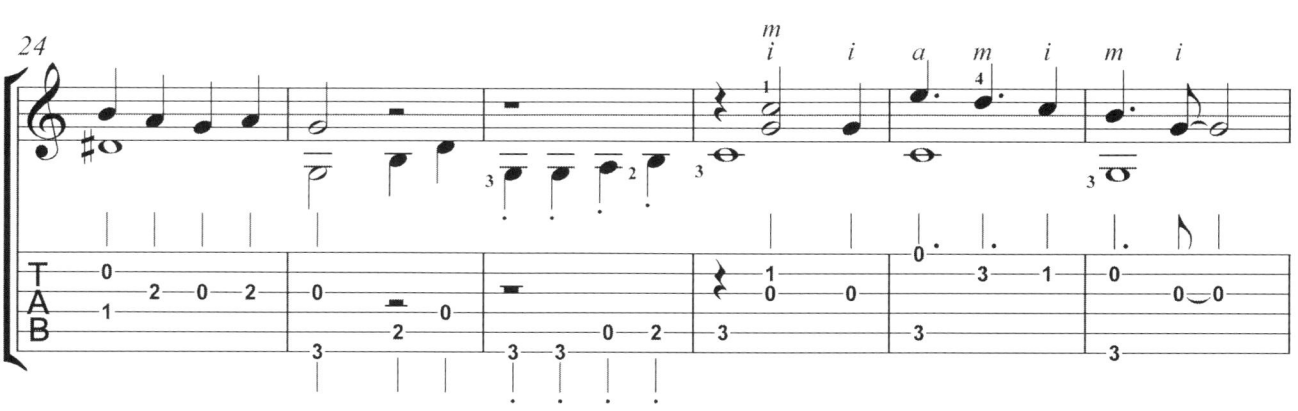
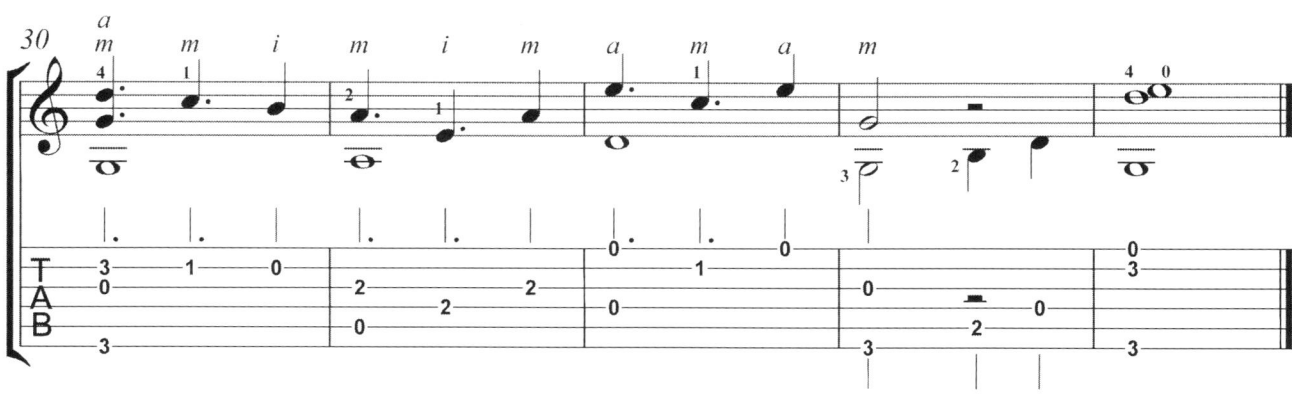

Eight Days A Week

Lennon/McCartney
Arr. by Javier Marco

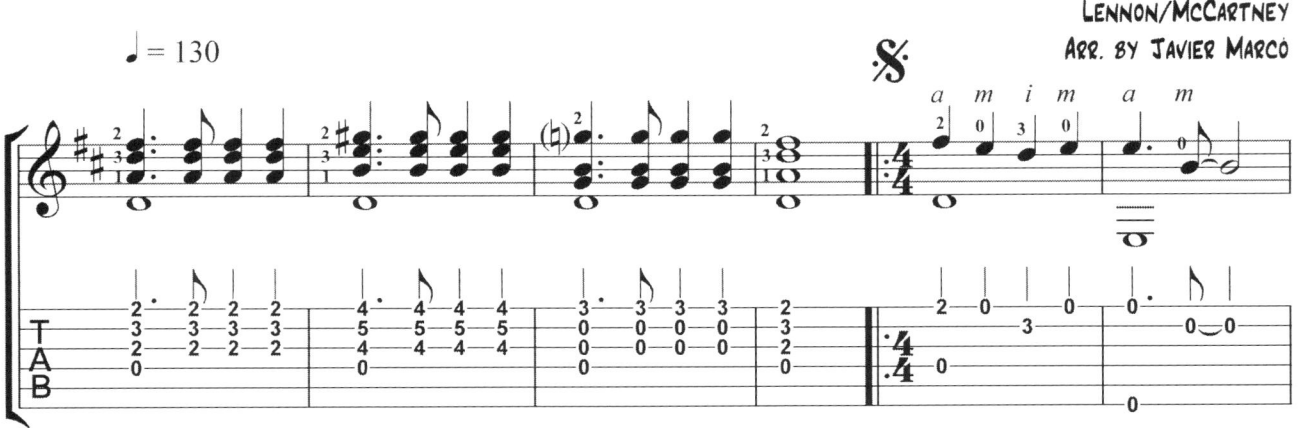
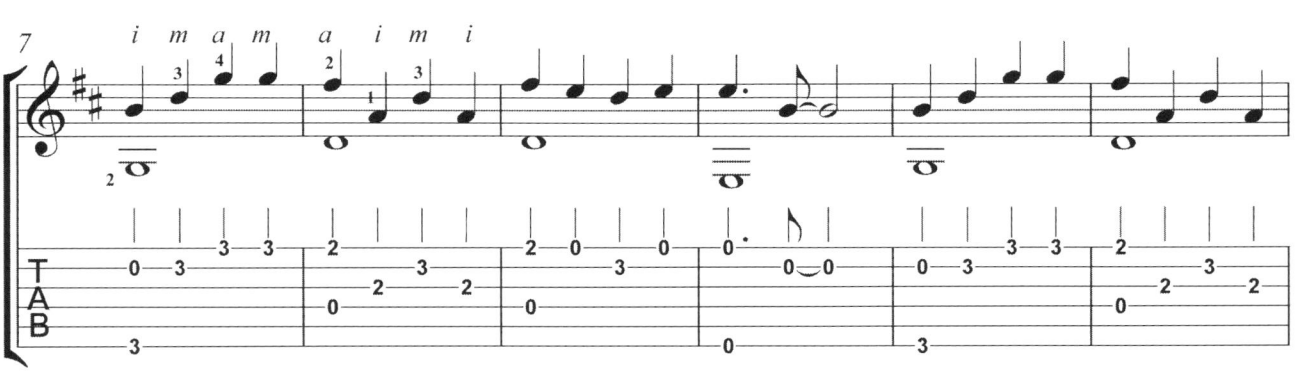

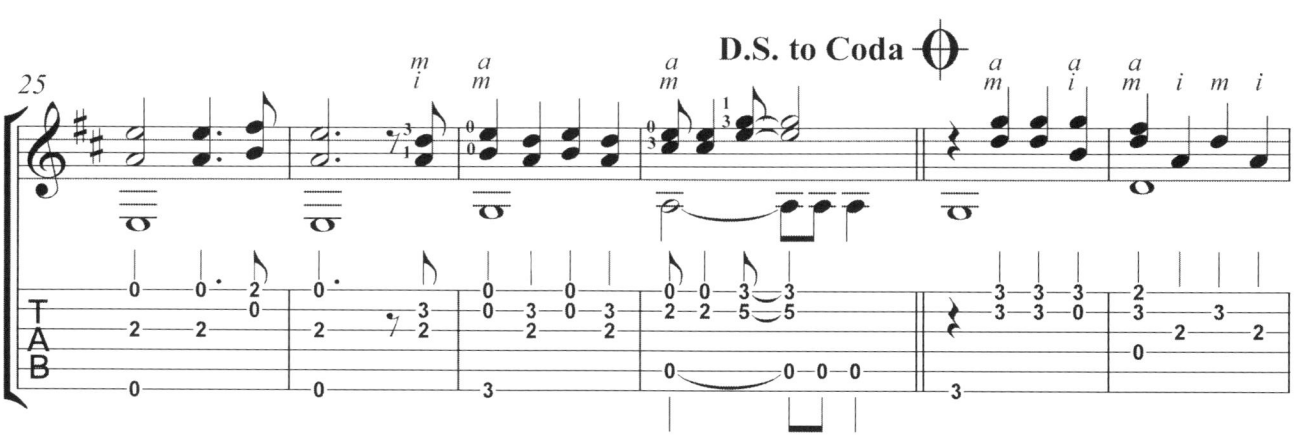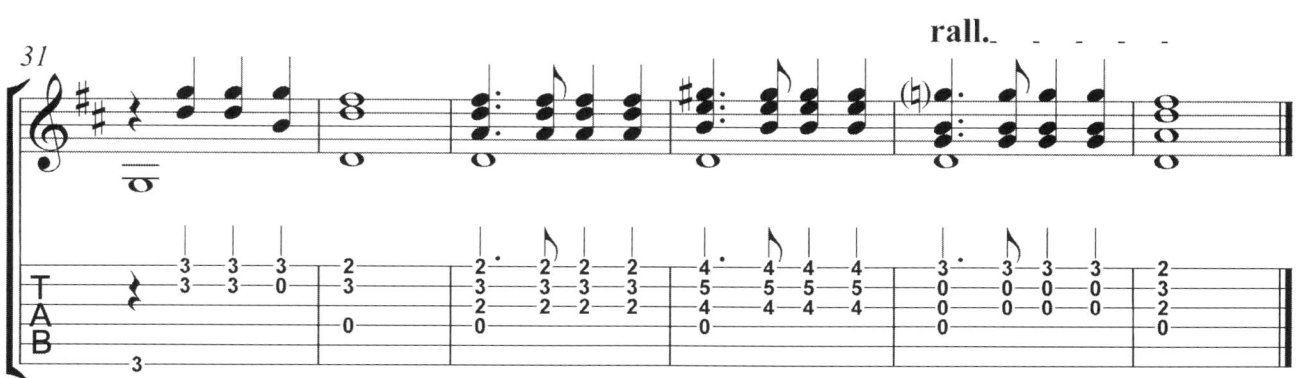

For No One

Lennon/McCartney
Arr. by Javier Marco

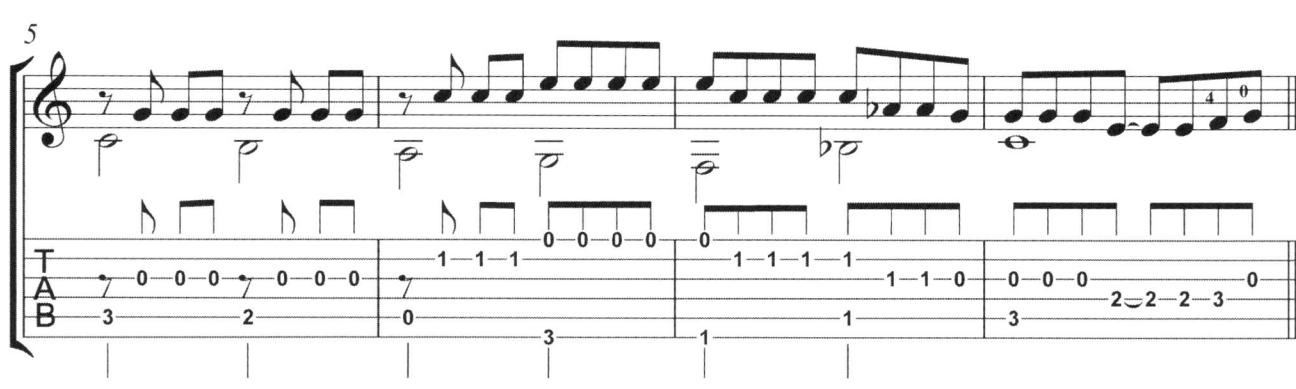

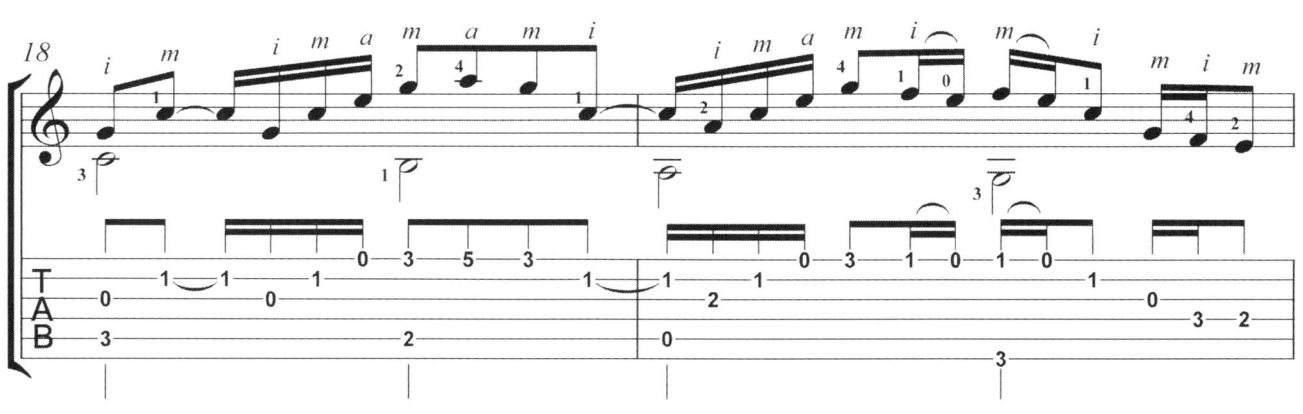

Help!

Lennon/McCartney
Arr. by Javier Marco

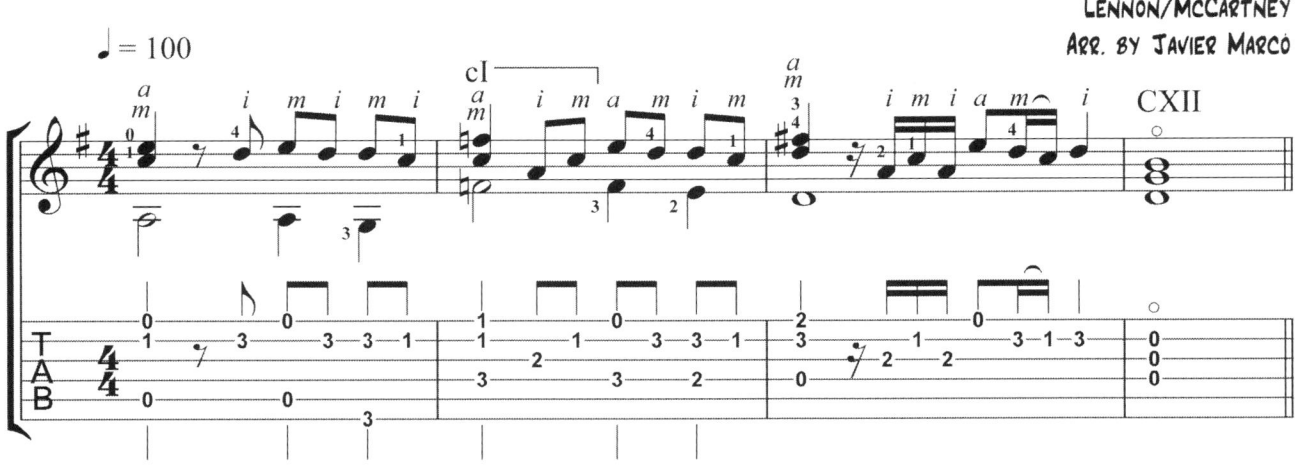
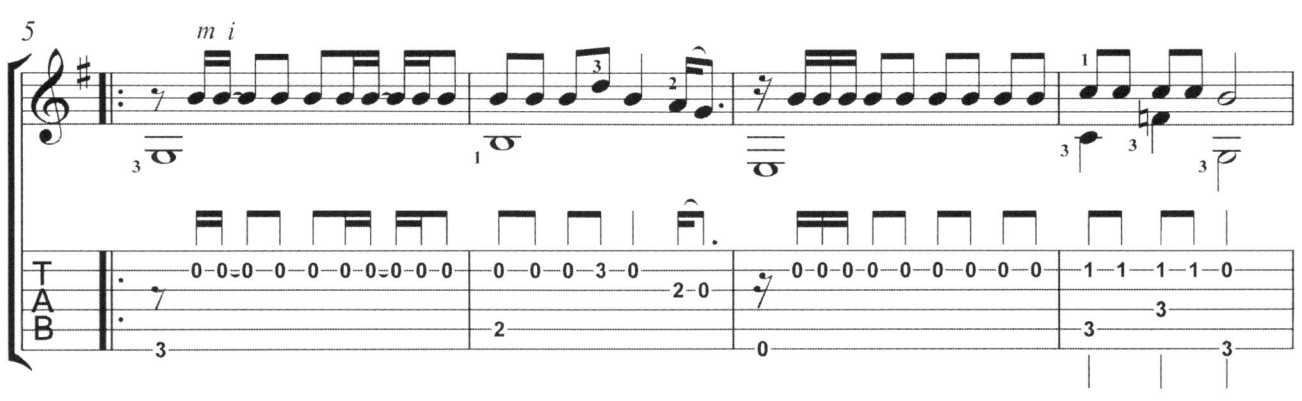
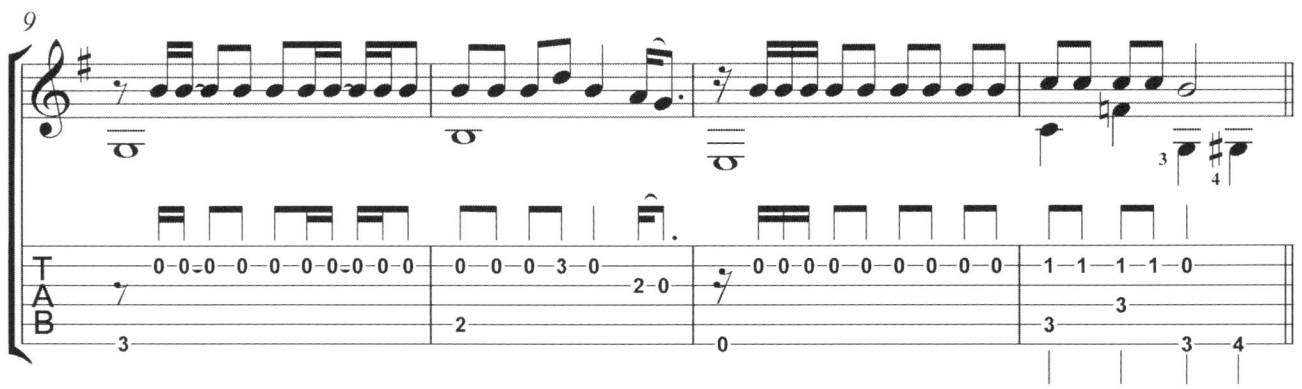

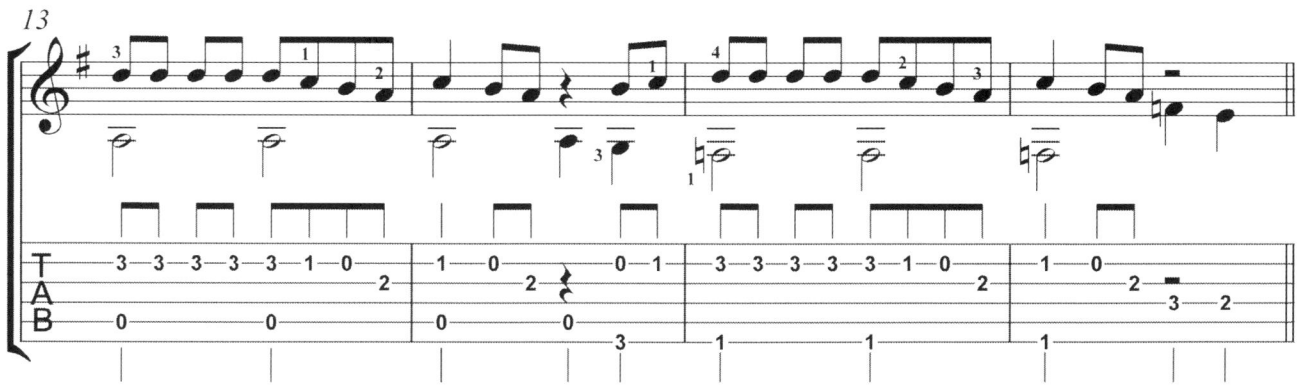
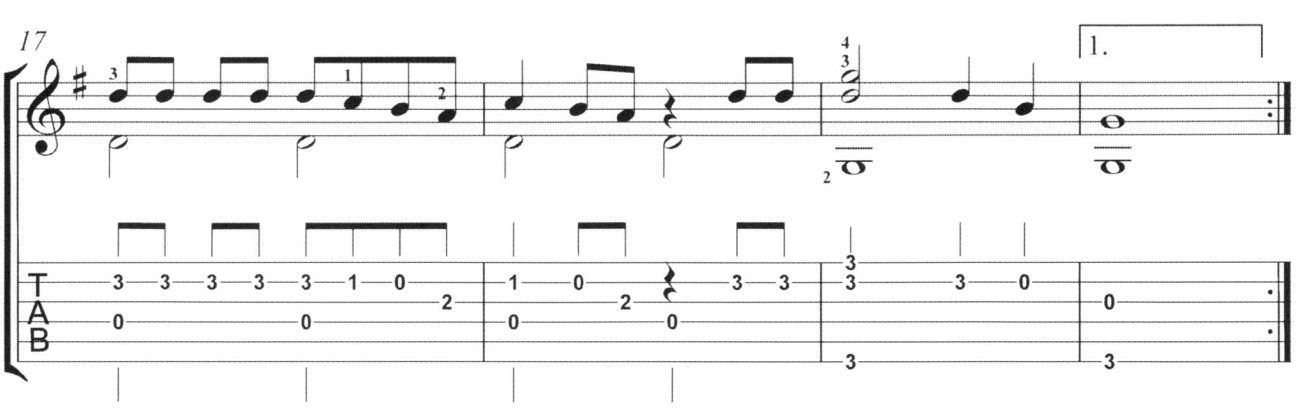

I Want To Hold Your Hand

Lennon/McCartney
Arr. by Javier Marco

I'll Follow The Sun

Lennon/McCartney
Arr. by Javier Marco

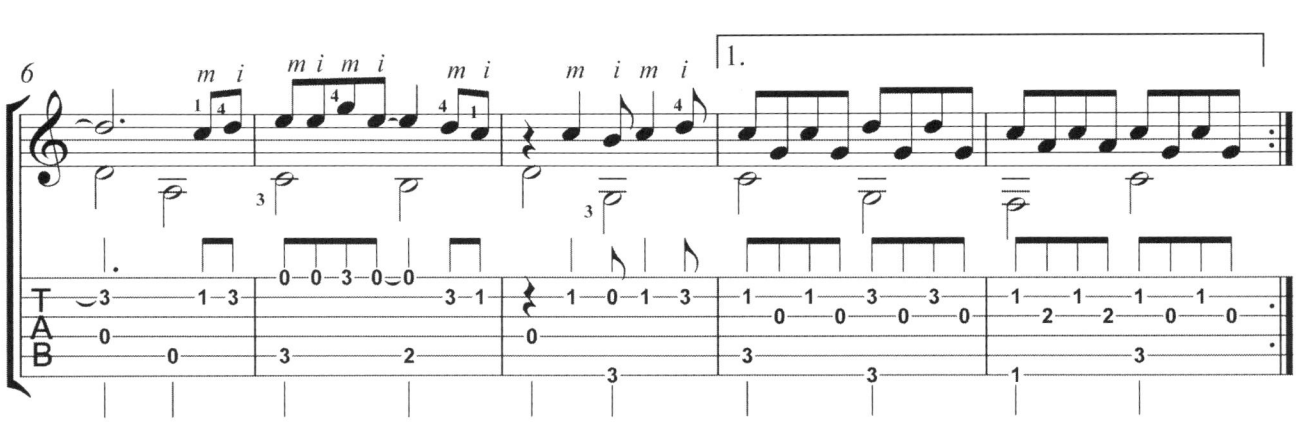
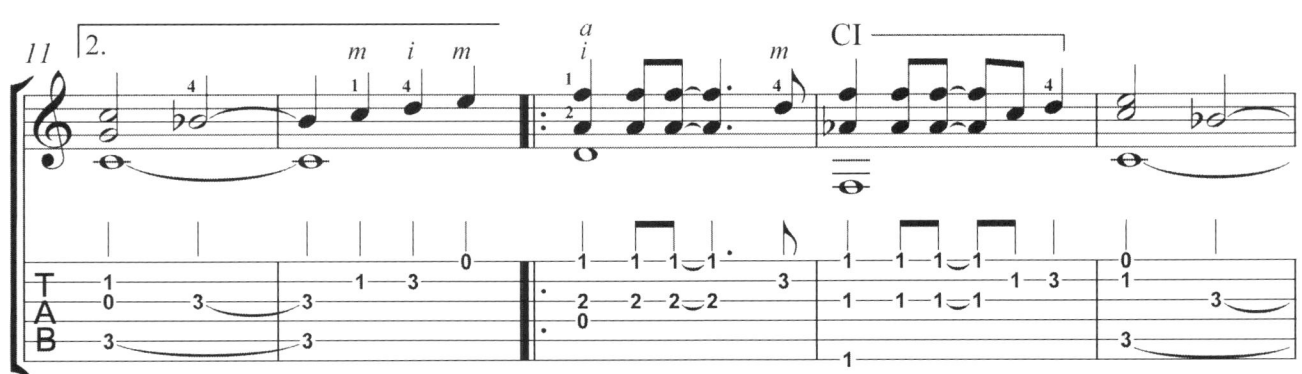

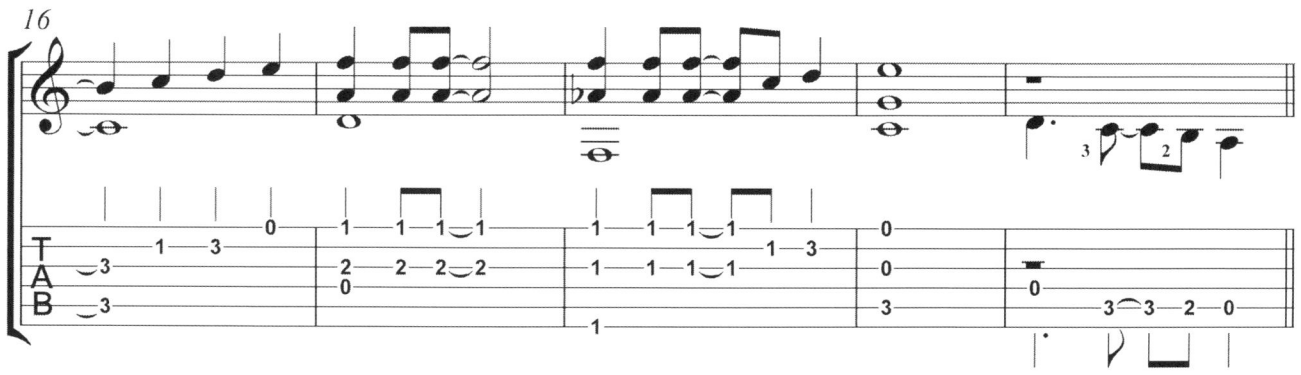
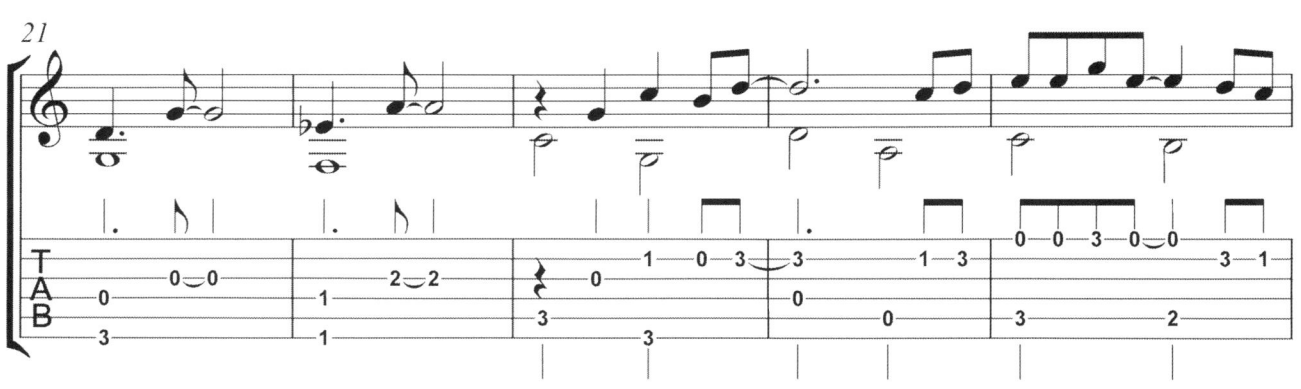
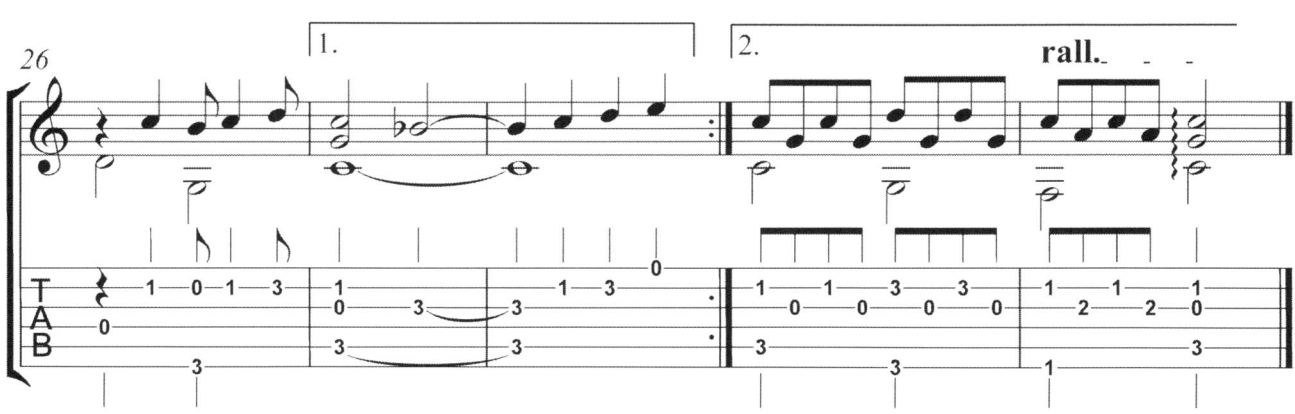

25

In My Life

Lennon/McCartney
Arr. by Javier Marco

It's Only Love

Lennon/McCartney
Arr. by Javier Marco

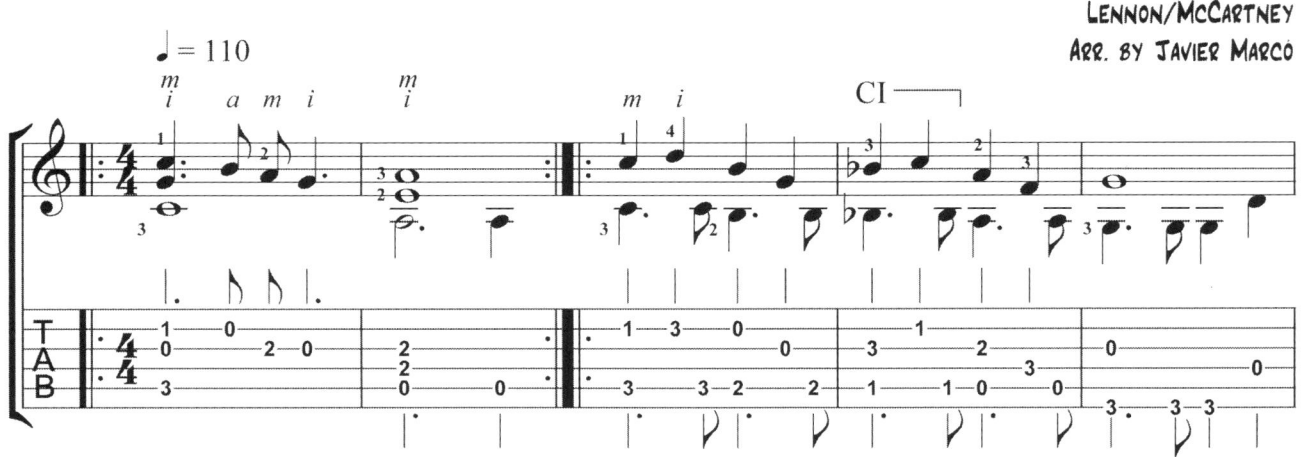
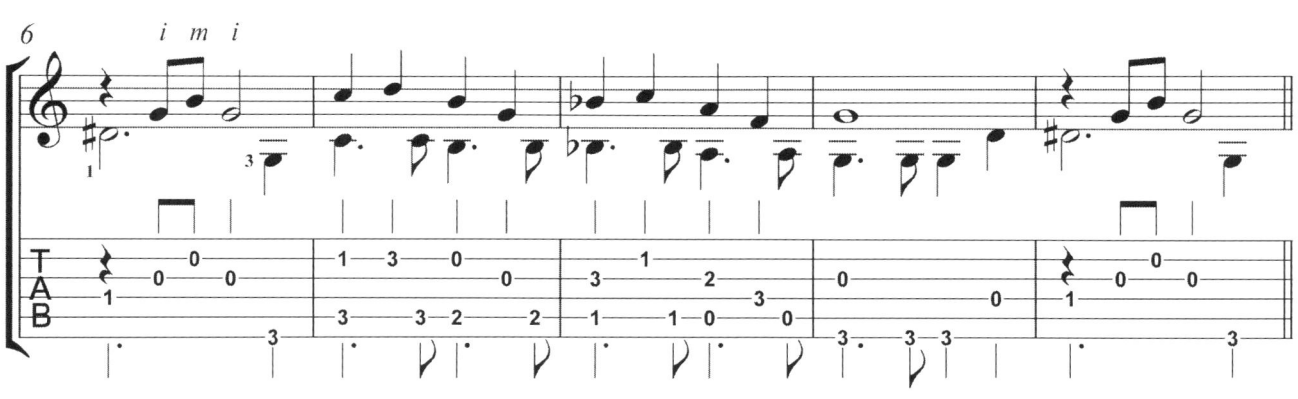
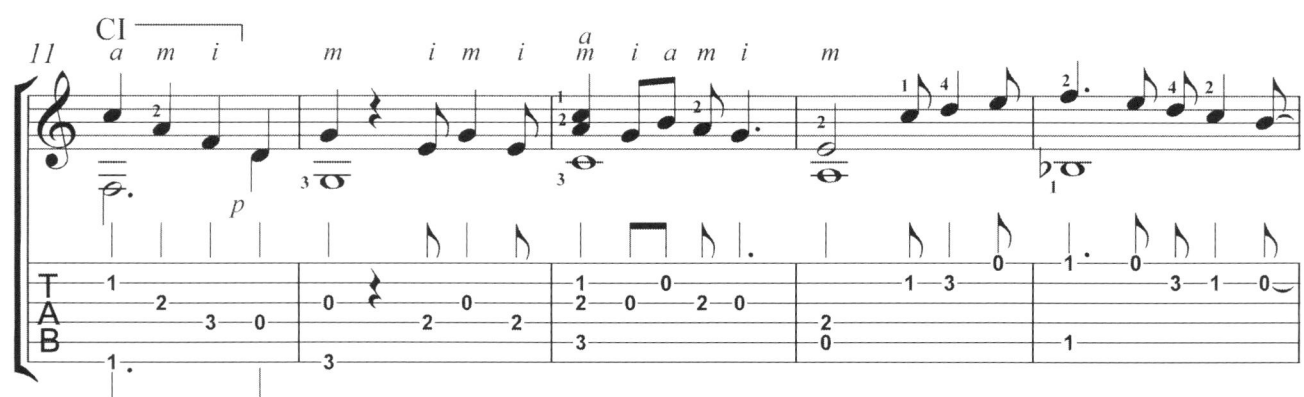

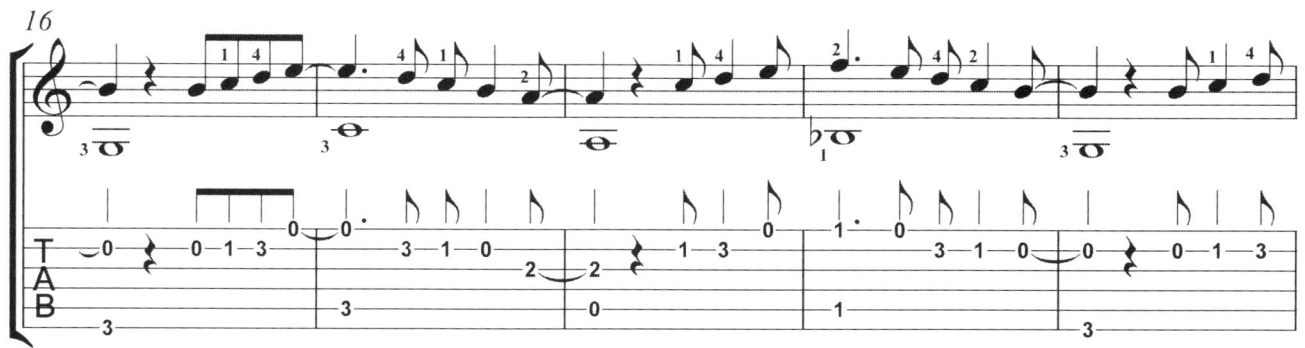
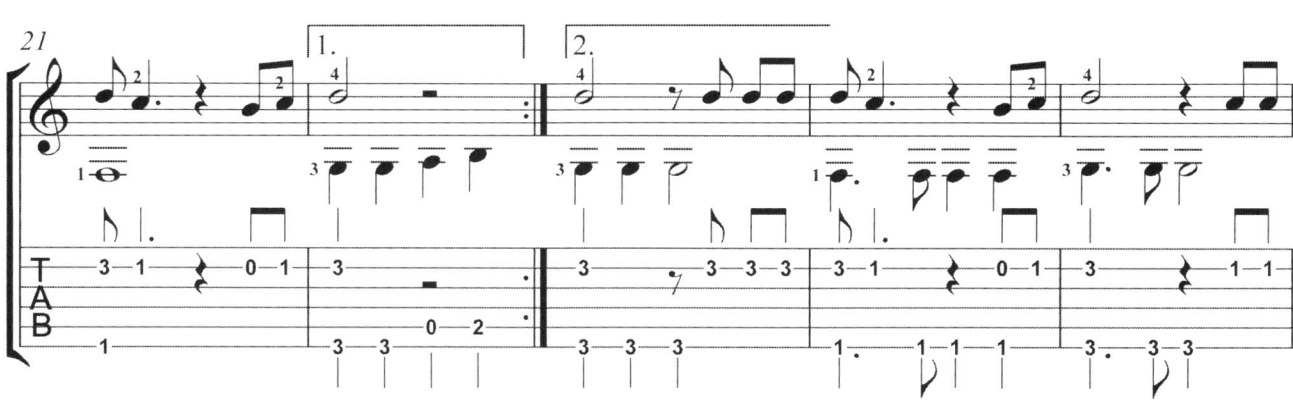
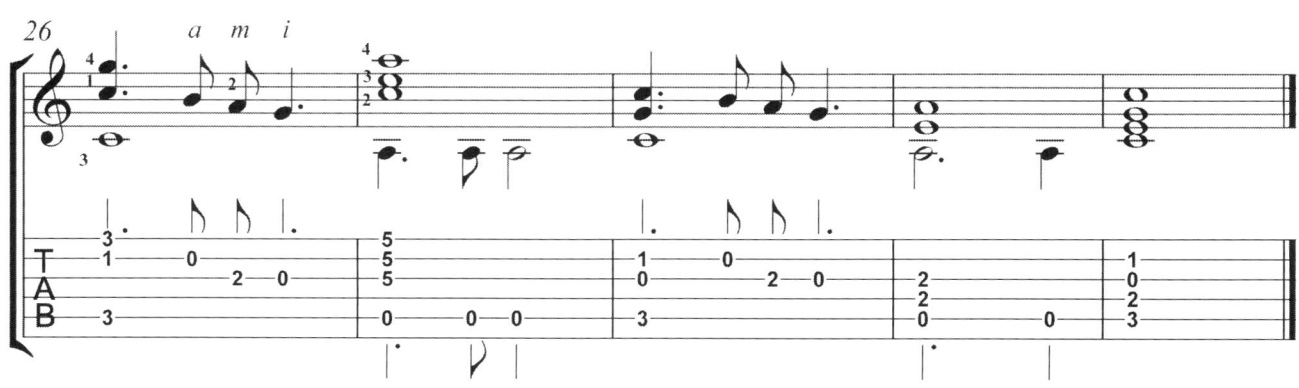

29

Lucy In The Sky With Diamonds

Lennon/McCartney
Arr. by Javier Marco

30

Nowhere Man

Lennon/McCartney
Arr. by Javier Marco

She's Leaving Home

Lennon/McCartney
Arr. by Javier Marco

The Long And Winding Road

Lennon/McCartney
Arr. by Javier Marco

36

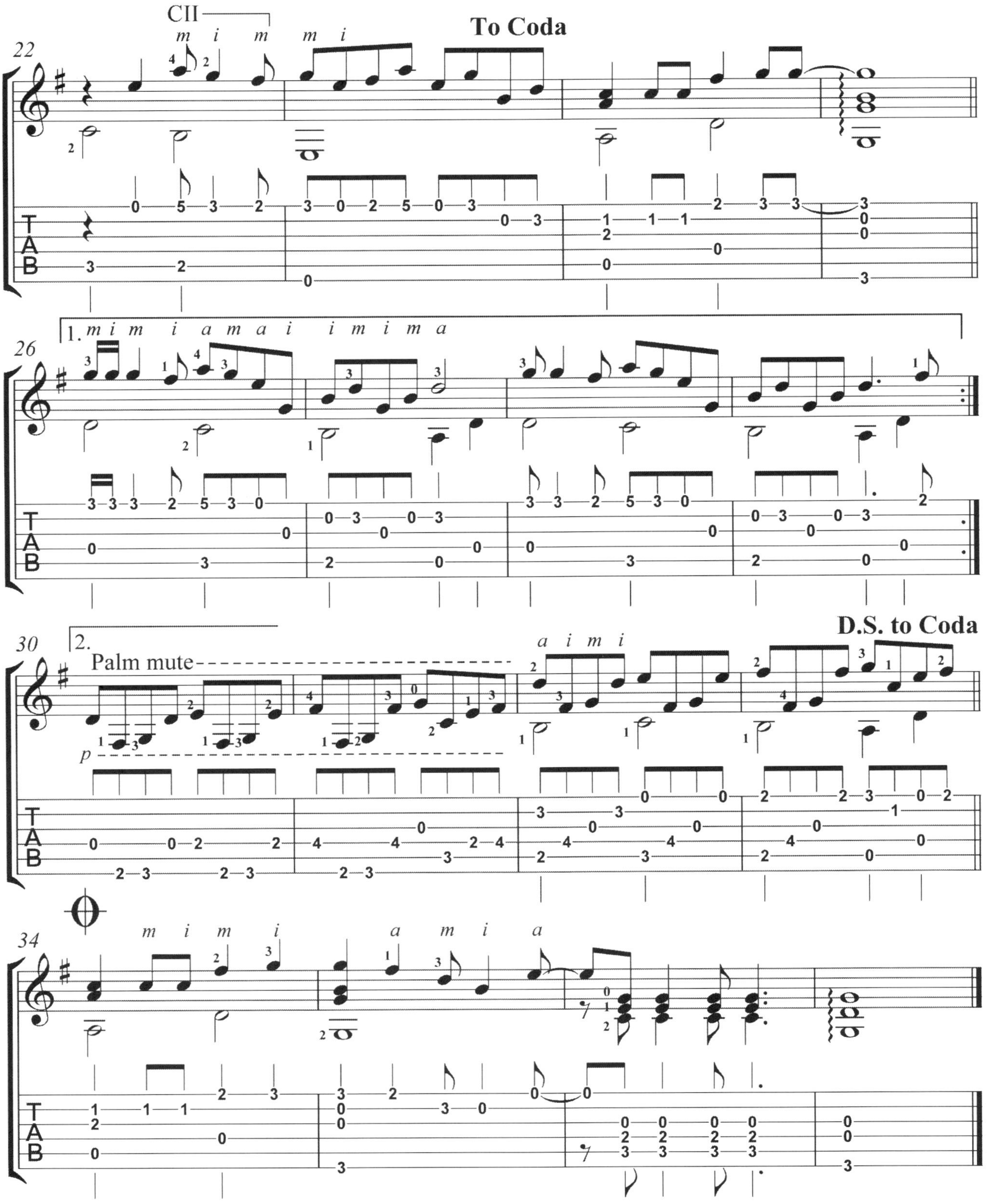
CII
To Coda
1.
2.
Palm mute
D.S. to Coda

While My Guitar Gently Weeps

Harrison
Arr. by Javier Marco

39

Yellow Submarine

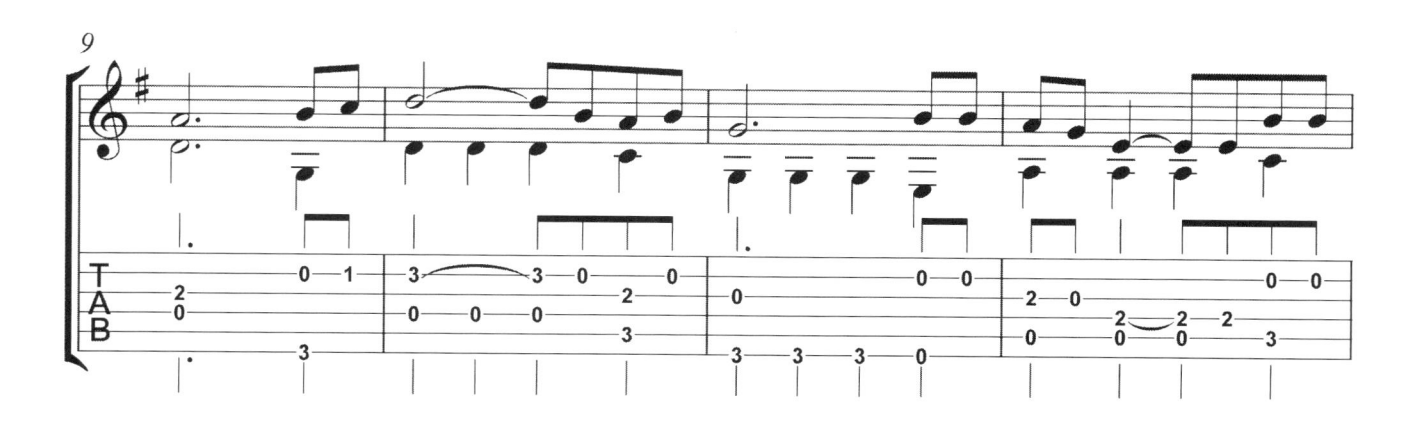

Lennon/McCartney
Arr. by Javier Marco

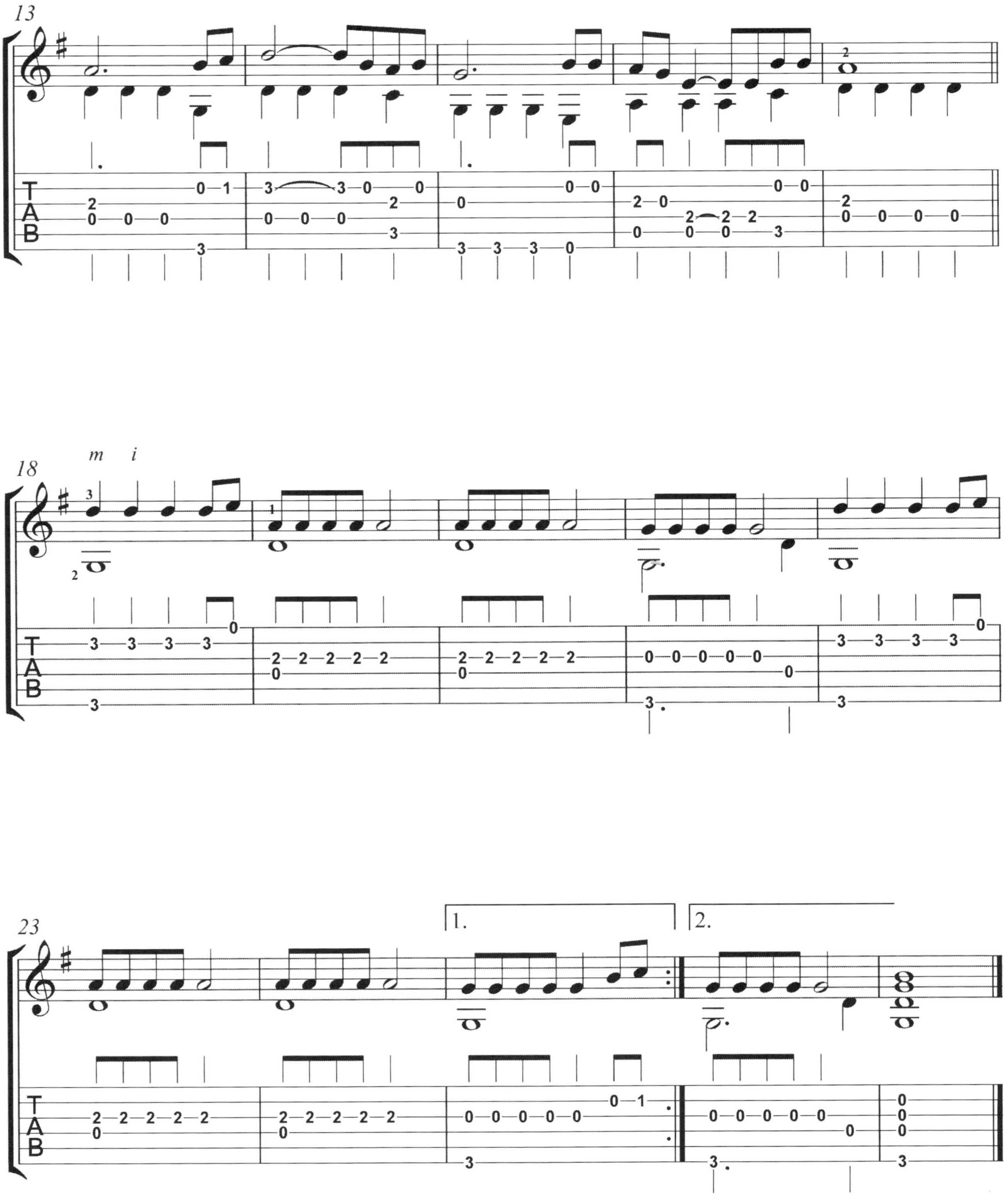
13
18
m i
23
1.
2.

SONGS IN STANDARD NOTATION

Across the Universe

Lennon/McCartney
Arr. by Javier Marco

All My Loving

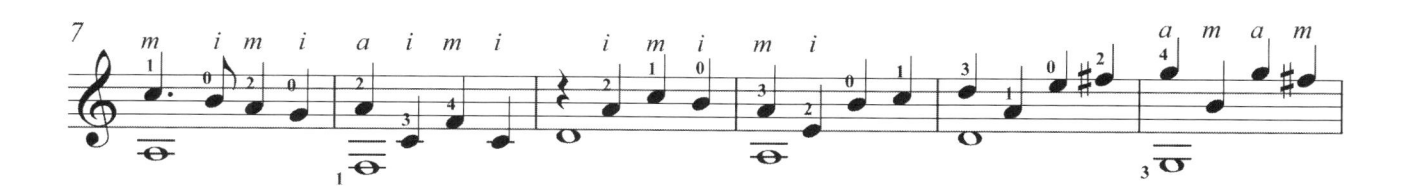

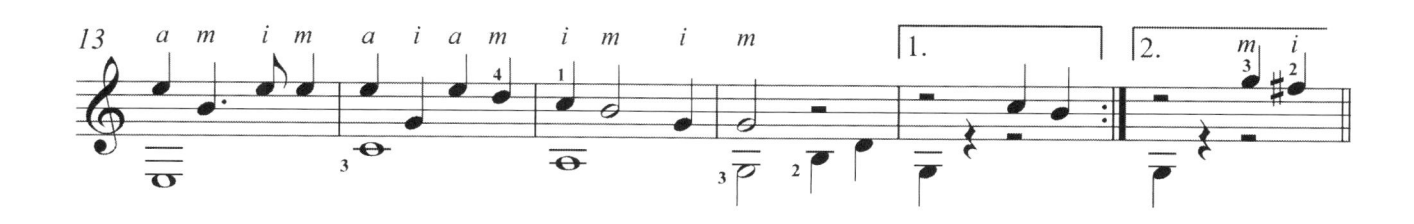

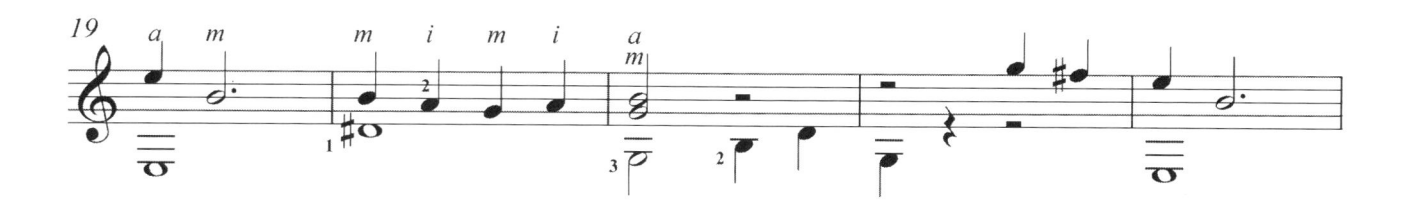

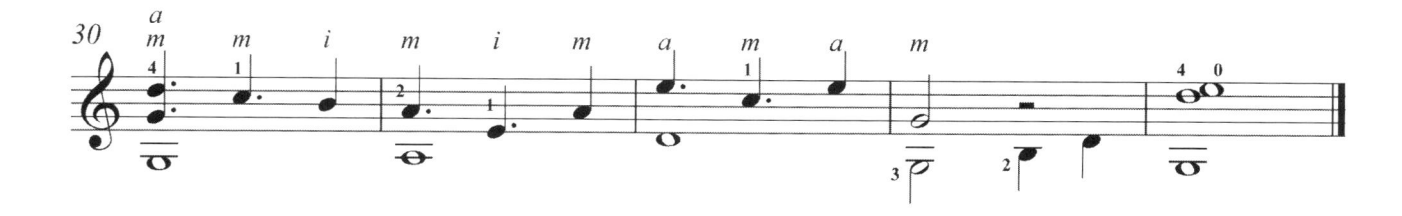

Lennon/McCartney
Arr. by Javier Marco

Eight Days A Week

Lennon/McCartney
Arr. by Javier Marco

For No One

Lennon/McCartney
Arr. by Javier Marco

Help!

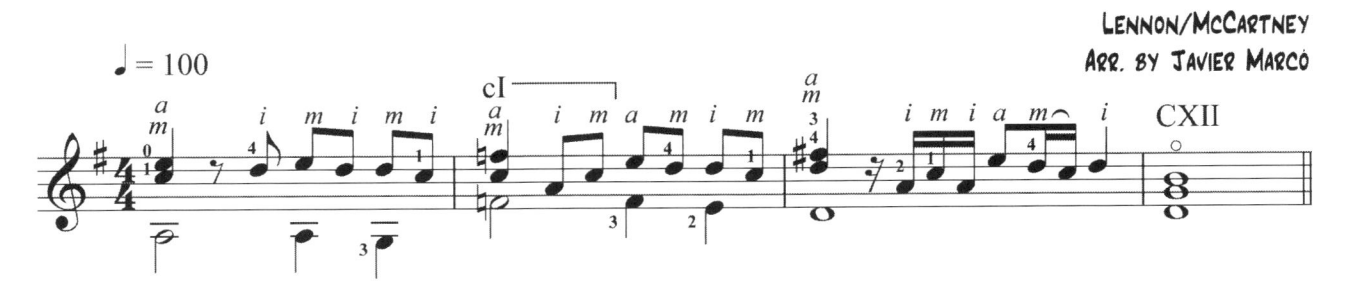

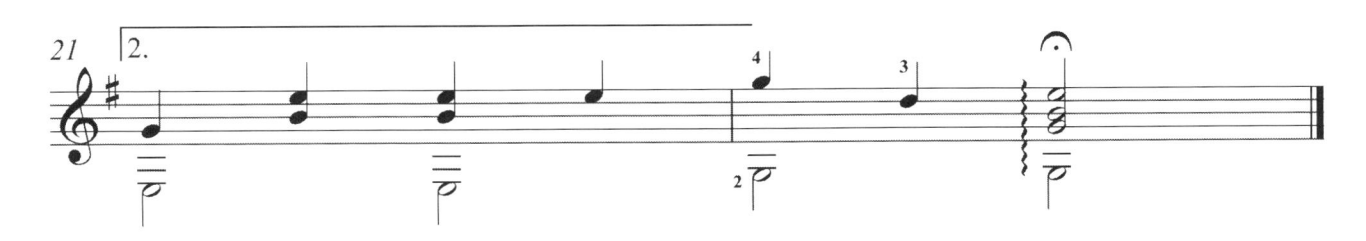

Lennon/McCartney
Arr. by Javier Marcó

I Want To Hold Your Hand

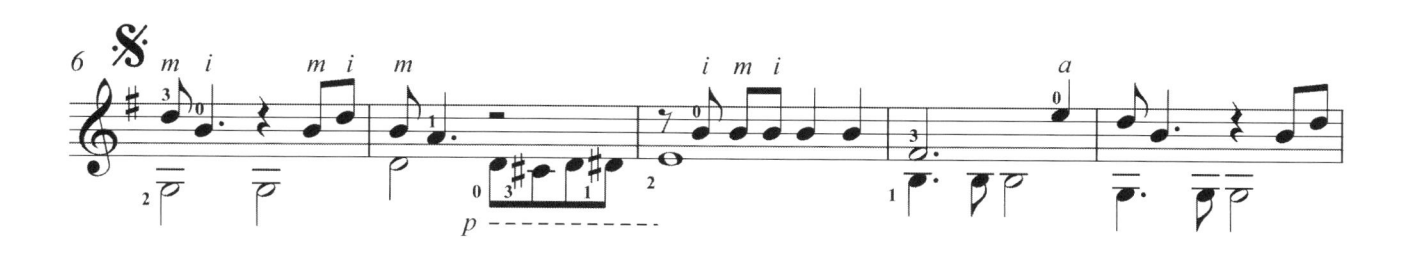

Lennon/McCartney
Arr. by Javier Marco

♩ = 130

51

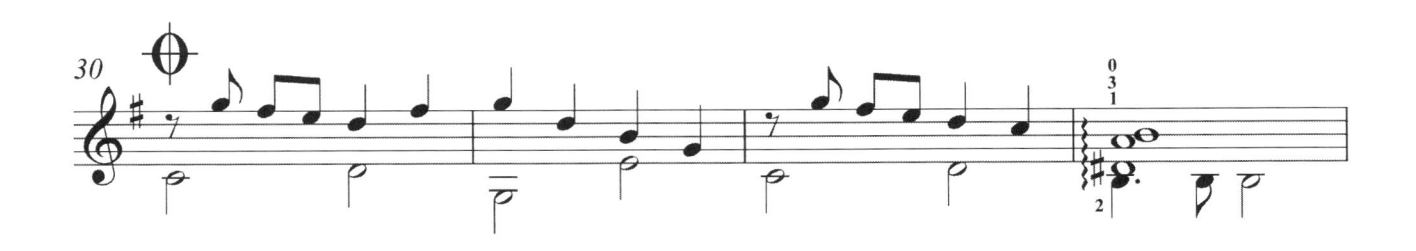

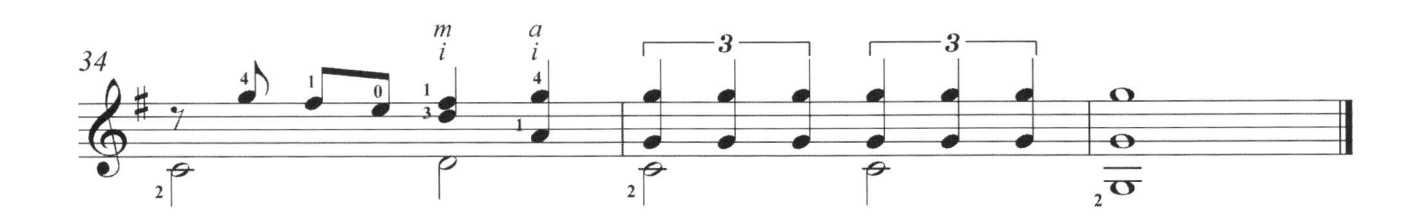

I'll Follow The Sun

Lennon/McCartney
Arr. by Javier Marco

It's Only Love

Lennon/McCartney
Arr. by Javier Marcó

In My Life

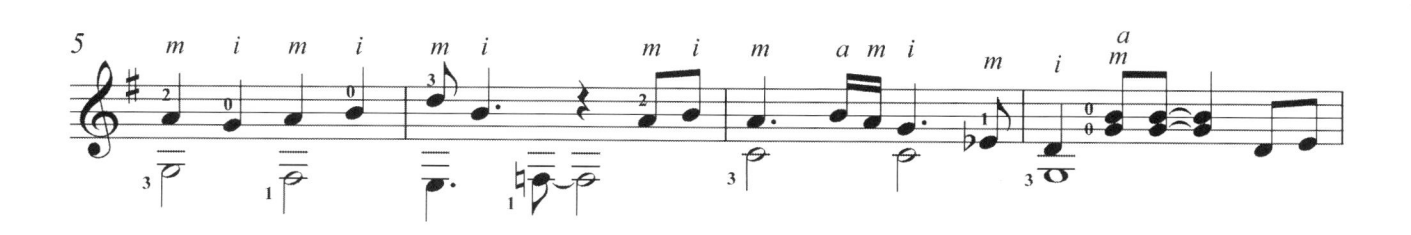

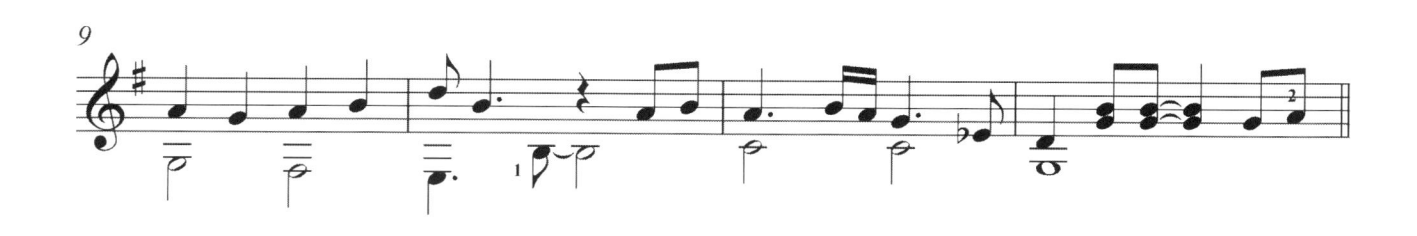

Lennon/McCartney
Arr. by Javier Marco

17
To Coda
21
m a m a m i m
i m m m i m
a
a m a m a m a i
m i m i m i m i
25
D. S. to Coda
a m i a m i m
29
rall.
a tempo
i m
p

Lucy In The Sky With Diamonds

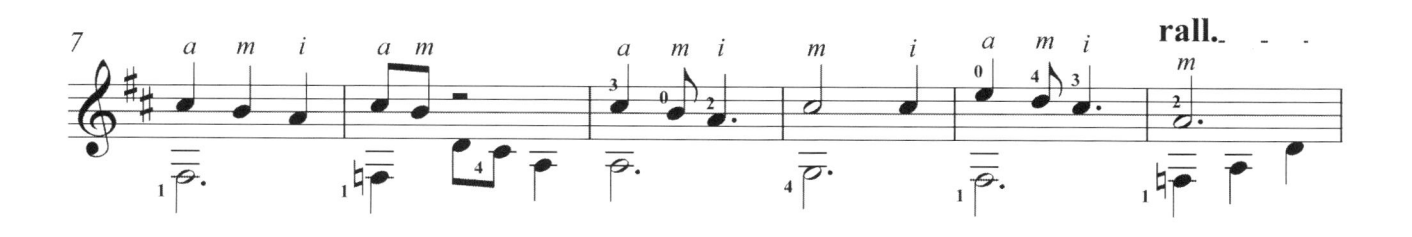

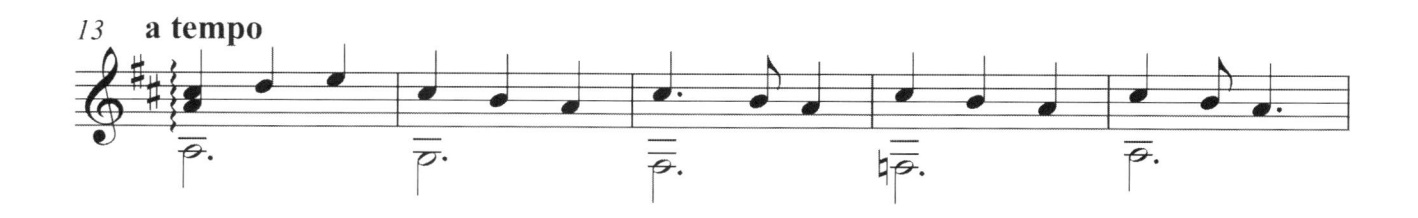

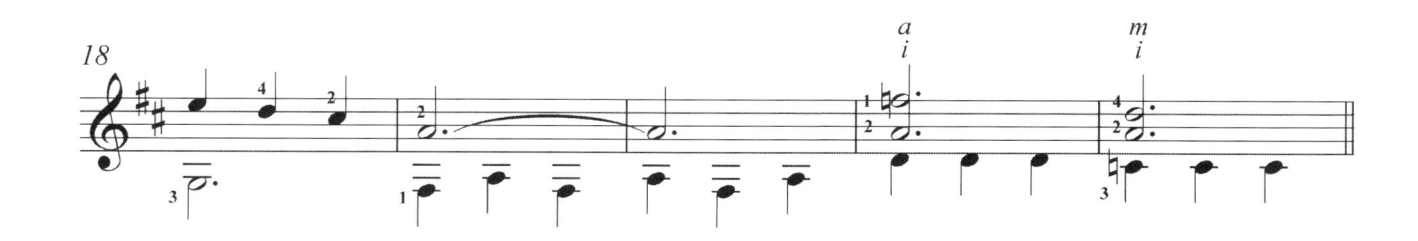

Lennon/McCartney
Arr. by Javier Marco

57

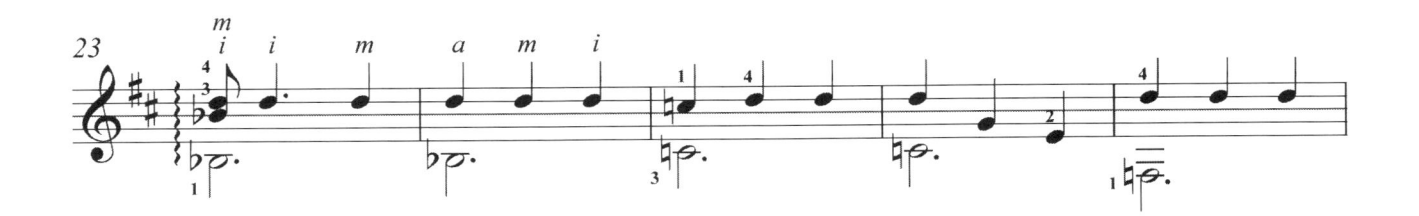

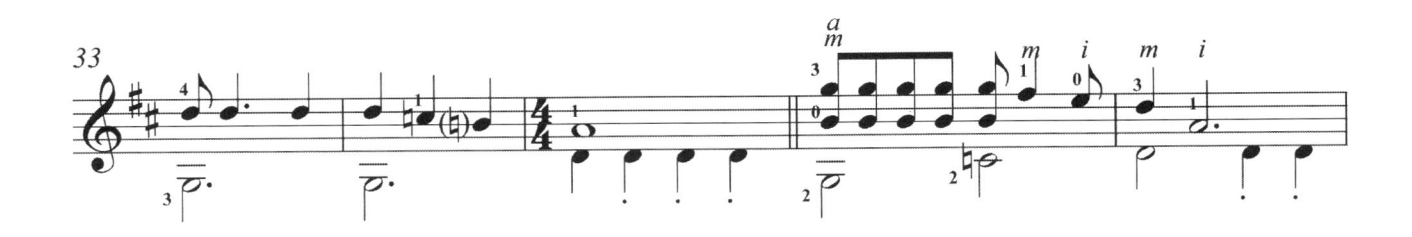

Nowhere Man

Lennon/McCartney
Arr. by Javier Marco

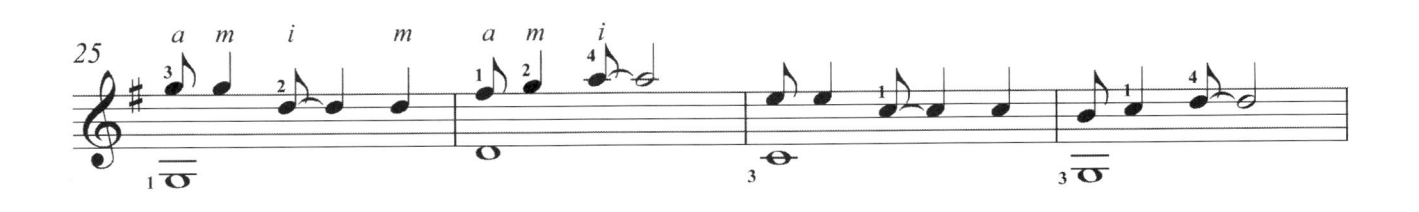

She's Leaving Home

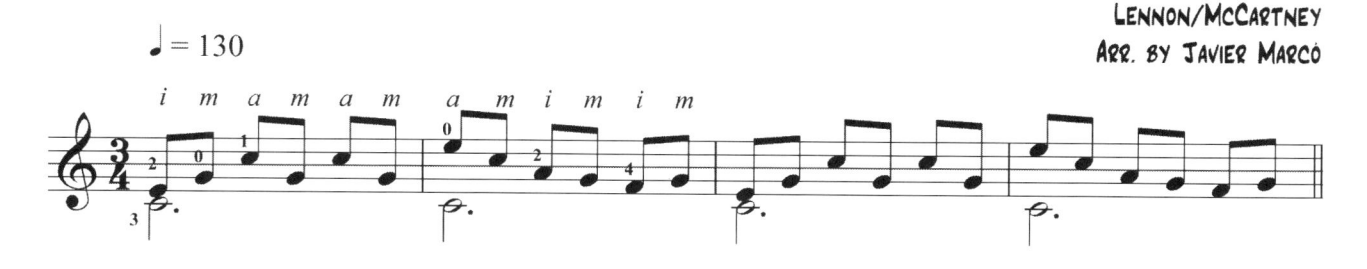

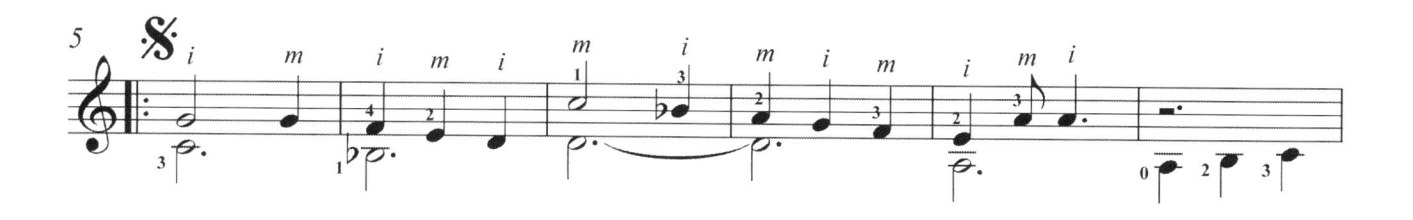

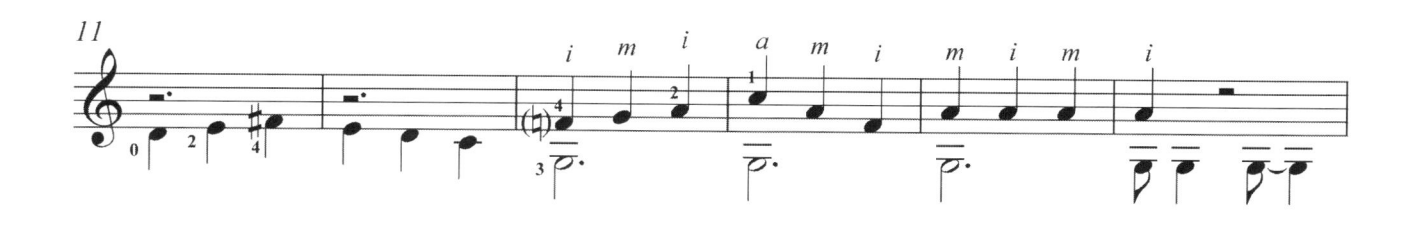

Lennon/McCartney
Arr. by Javier Marco

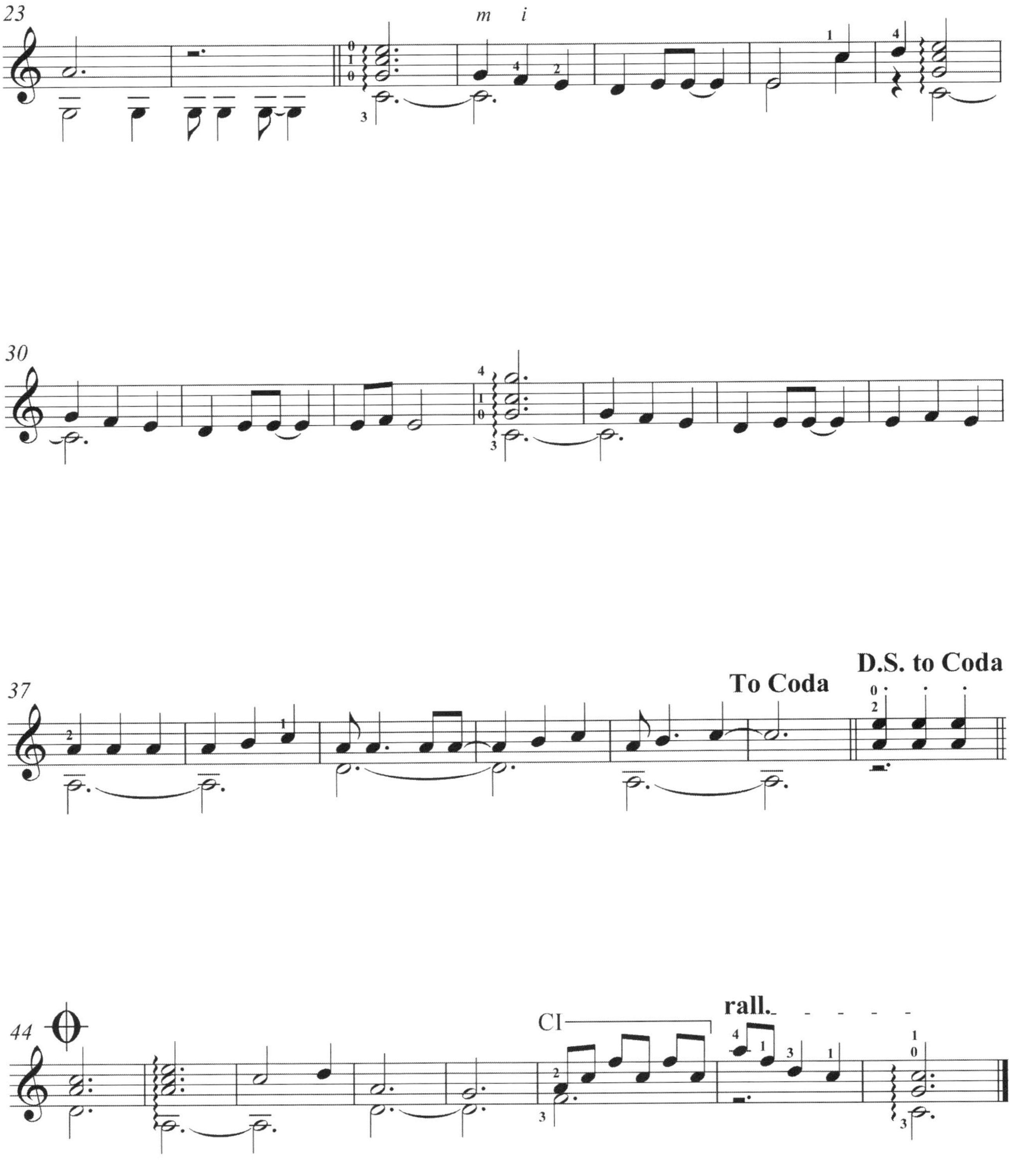
23
m i
30
37
To Coda
D.S. to Coda
44
CI
rall.

The Long And Winding Road

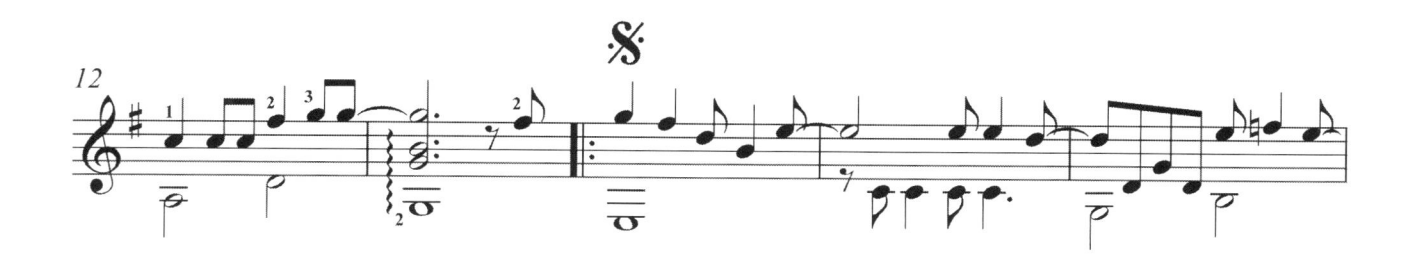

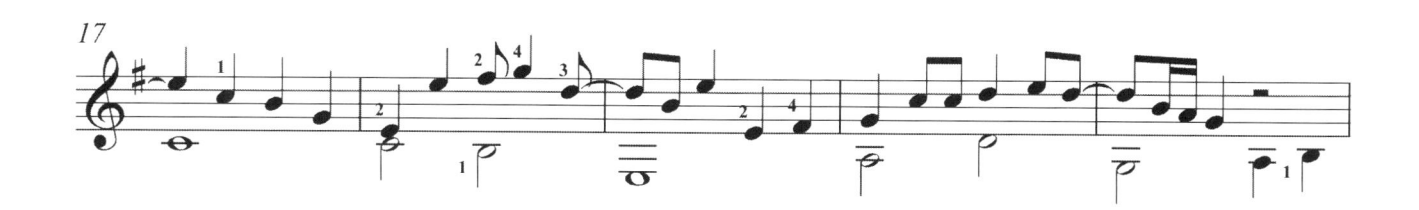

Lennon/McCartney
Arr. by Javier Marco

22
CII
m i m m i
To Coda
26
1. m i m i a m a i i m i m a
30
2.
Palm mute
p
a i m i
D.S. to Coda
34
m i m i
a m i a

While My Guitar Gently Weeps

Harrison
Arr. by Javier Marco

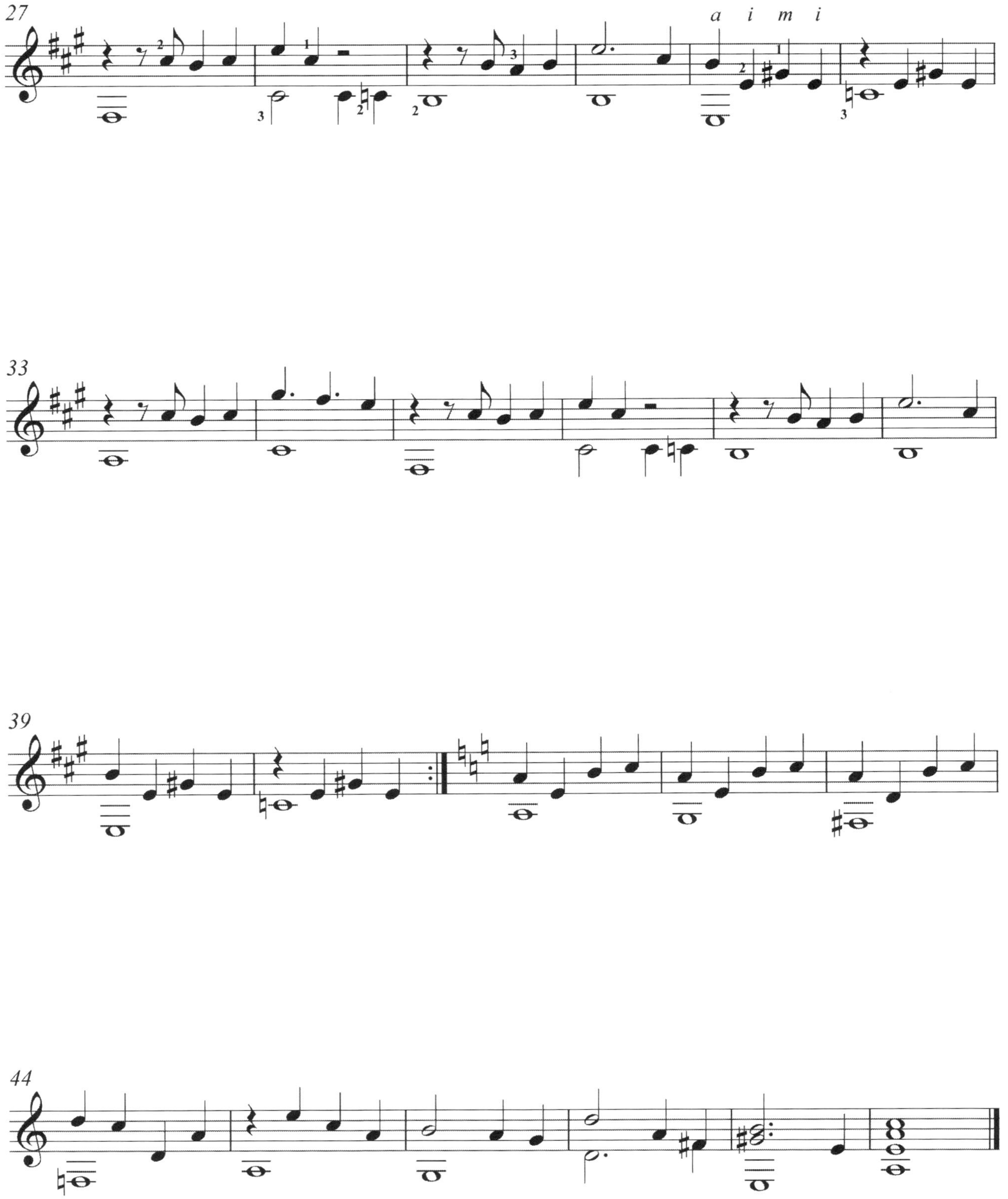
27
a i m i
33
39
44

Yellow Submarine

Lennon/McCartney
Arr. by Javier Marco

WE HOPE YOU HAVE ENJOYED THE SHOW!
SGT PEPPERS
LONELY HEARTS
CLUB BAND

Made in the USA
San Bernardino, CA
18 November 2013